"Pastor McGowan la
the church's use of the imprecatory psalms. He clearly shows that the Old and New Testaments are not opposed to each other concerning the love of enemies and the seeking of God's justice. With wisdom and humility, he answers the difficult question concerning how the church can use the imprecatory psalms today. I highly recommend this work."

–DR. RICHARD P. BELCHER, JR.,
PROFESSOR OF OLD TESTAMENT AND ACADEMIC DEAN
REFORMED THEOLOGICAL SEMINARY, CHARLOTTE

"Pastor McGowan has done a masterful job of presenting, clearly and succinctly, the theology and purpose of that body of psalms which are commonly maligned or embarrassingly ignored: the psalms that curse. Why are they in the Bible? How can a believer pray them—if he or she may properly pray them at all? Pastor McGowan has distilled their essence and steers us in a path toward a helpful and hopeful embrace of these prayers once again. May the Lord use this work to embolden the church to both live and pray for 'Thy kingdom come, Thy will be done.'"

–DR. JOHN N. DAY,
AUTHOR OF CRYING FOR JUSTICE: WHAT THE PSALMS
TEACH US ABOUT MERCY AND VENGEANCE IN AN AGE
OF TERRORISM

i

"*In this very helpful introduction to the imprecatory psalms, Sean McGowan has achieved the all too rare virtues of both brevity and substantiveness, of both popular accessibility and scholarly precision, of both pastoral winsomeness and prophetic urgency. I highly commend it to you.*"

–GEORGE GRANT,
PASTOR OF PARISH PCA, FRANKLIN, TN

"*This tiny book comes in fast, focused, and fastidious as it addresses several significant questions. It answers if the psalms that present 'harsh language' and make us uncomfortable at times still have any relevance for the church today and ought they to even be used in prayers by the church in our age. McGowan makes convincing arguments in one direction and responds to several doubts in thoughtful ways. Psalms that Curse: A Brief Primer should be in the hands of every pastor and parishioner.*"

–REV. DR. MICHAEL W. PHILLIBER,
PASTOR OF HERITAGE PRESBYTERIAN CHURCH IN OKLAHOMA CITY AND AUTHOR OF *OUR HEADS ON STRAIGHT: SOBER-MINDEDNESS—A FORGOTTEN CHRISTIAN VIRTUE*

"Bible-believing Christians recognize God's Word to be a unified, harmonious, and coherent revelation of His character and creation. So what do we do with harsh or difficult passages such as the curses we read in the imprecatory psalms? Surely we cannot omit these verses in our devotions, singing, teaching, or praying. But they present a unique challenge to us when we think about how to apply them. My friend Pastor Sean McGowan has ably written a straight-forward guide to orient our thinking about the imprecatory psalms and to defend the propriety of their use in our spiritual lives."

–Rev. Zachary Groff,
pastor of Antioch Presbyterian Church
(PCA) in Woodruff, SC

PSALMS THAT CURSE

A BRIEF PRIMER

SEAN McGOWAN

FOREWORD BY DR. BENJAMIN SHAW

Psalms that Curse: A Brief Primer
© 2021 Sean McGowan
Published by Reformation Zion Publishing
Ann Arbor, MI
www.reformationzion.com

Published 2021
Printed in the United States of America
ISBN: 978-1-956521-04-7

Contents

FOREWORD

There is a subgroup of psalms that most people like to avoid. They say nasty things about enemies and wish horrible things upon them. They are generally referred to as imprecatory psalms, from imprecation, meaning a spoken curse. Many Christian writers who deal with them treat them as somehow sub-Christian. The *Pulpit Commentary*, commenting on Psalm 35, says, "they give us, not God's precept, but man's defective prayers." Sam Storms helpfully pulls together a string of similar quotations.[1] These quotations come from notable and respected Christian authors. What are we to make of these psalms? Do they belong to the old dispensation? Have they passed away like the food laws so that we may safely ignore them?

These are difficult questions, and they demand answers. In this short book, Mr. McGowan takes a careful look at these psalms. He examines not only their content, which provokes the strong reactions

---

1. Sam Storms, "Imprecations in the Psalms," https://www.samstorms.org/all-articles/post/imprecations-in-the-psalms-.

already mentioned, but their context. Where do they fit, not only in the book of Psalms but in the Bible as a whole? This careful study, which considers these psalms in their full biblical-theological context, is clear and helpful. Mr. McGowan's work reflects hard academic labor, but he presents the results of his study to the layperson without the academic impediments.

I highly recommend this work for the education and edification of the body of Christ.

Benjamin Shaw,
Professor of Old Testament
Reformation Bible College

INTRODUCTION

It is late at night. You are about to retire for the evening before you get a call from the senior pastor. He asks you to fill in at the local jail tomorrow where your church has been ministering to inmates for a long time. He tells you that he has been going through the Psalms and the next installment will be Psalm 58. Although you have not had your seminary class on the Psalms just yet, you figure since you have read through them enough you should be fine. You tell him that you would love to fill in and call it a night.

You finally arrive at the prison and are greeted by the guards who quickly bring you to the study room. After fellowshipping with the inmates, you learn that many of them had a violent past and are new Christians. Thanking God for hearing these wonderful testimonies, you begin your lesson. Then it hits you... Psalm 58:6 jumps out. "O God, break the teeth in their mouths; tear out the fangs of the young lions O LORD!" It continues: "Let them be like the snail that dissolves into slime, like the stillborn child who never sees the sun" (Ps. 58:8). One of the inmates raises his hand and asks the obvious question: "Why is this in the Bible?" "This sounds an awful lot like how we would talk when we wanted to take vengeance on our enemies." It gets worse. Another inmate begins searching the Psalms and quickly zones in on another passage: "Blessed is he who takes your little ones and dashes them against the rock!" "Pastor" he asks, "How can this be coming from the word of God?"

Unfortunately for this pastor-in-training, these verses were new to him. For many Christians, their reaction is similar to that of this young man. They either have never read these particular psalms, or if they have, they are not sure how to understand them. Perhaps some in their more honest moments would react in horror: "How in the world could the Bible call someone 'blessed' that dashes infants against the rocks?"

It is my hope that this short primer will give those that have trouble with these specific texts some suggested guidelines for how to understand them. While a topic like this covers much ground, our outline will be simple. We will explore the background to these psalms, work through one of the most challenging of them, Psalm 137, and then ask whether or not these psalms can be uttered by Christians in any context today. It is my desire that this little work will give you the tools to navigate and grapple with these particular words of Scripture.

CHAPTER 1

A CURSORY GLANCE
AT THE PSALMS

BEFORE WE BEGIN to work through these kinds of psalms, it is important to take a step back and build a foundational understanding of the Psalms in general. The Psalms played a pivotal role in the life of the nation of Israel and were composed over a long period of time. These psalms that have been handed down to us were not written in one setting, or even by one author, but are a collection of individual psalms that were penned by people like Moses (Ps. 90), as well as authors living after the exile (Ps. 126). Nearly spanning a 1,000-year period of time, the historical background of the Psalms is the history of the nation of Israel.[1]

---

1. Tremper Longman III and Raymond B. Dillard, *An Introduction to the Old Testament* (Grand Rapids: Zondervan, 2004), 239.

Author(s)/Compiler

An important distinction that needs to be made in understanding the composition of the psalms is that between the writing of the *individual* psalm and the compilation of the collection *as a whole*. We know that someone later on, after the exile, compiled the entire Psalter into what eventually came to be the five-book structure we have in our Bibles. We know from the titles[2] that there were a number of different authors of these psalms, with David being a significant contributor.

The book of Psalms played an important role in the worship of Israel, specifically in the temple and in the synagogue (which developed after the destruction of the first temple in 586 B.C.). In fact, many of the prayers and songs that were utilized in synagogue worship were taken from the Psalter.[3] Given the central role of the Psalms in the worship of Israel, it should come as no surprise that

---

2. There has been considerable debate over whether the titles were original to the composition of the psalms. Some have argued the titles were original. Others have argued that they reflect an early, reliable tradition, but should not be taken as original or inspired. And still others disregard them all together. For further discussion, see Gleason L. Archer, *A Survey of Old Testament Introduction* (Chicago: Moody Press, 1964), 491–493; Longman and Dillard, *An Introduction to the Old Testament*, 239–244; Bruce K. Waltke, *An Old Testament Theology* (Grand Rapids: Zondervan, 2007), 871–881.

3. Philip Schaff, *History of the Christian Church*, vol. 1 (Peabody: Hendricksen, 1858), 458.

the early church inherited this hymn book as their own. Not only do we see Jesus and the disciples participating in the great psalm-singing as part of the Passover liturgy in Matthew 26:30, but other New Testament examples show where believers were exhorted to sing psalms in the corporate worship of the church.

In Ephesians 5:18-19, Paul exhorts Christians not to get drunk with wine but to be "filled with the Spirit, addressing one another in psalms and hymns and spiritual songs, singing and making melody to the Lord with your heart" (see also Col. 3:16). What this imperative shows us is that, at the very least, the Psalter was expected to be used in early Christian worship.

To the early Christians, in contrast to today's hymns, the Psalms were the Word of the living God. The New Testament church had a very high view of the Old Testament, understanding it to be *God-breathed* (2 Tim. 3:16) and written down by men who were "carried along by the Holy Spirit" (2 Pet. 1:21). Given the fact that the Psalms were part of the third section of the Hebrew Bible called the "Writings," their view of the Psalter would not have been any different. In fact, we see as much in the pages of the New Testament itself. For example, before quoting Psalm 110, Jesus notes that "David himself *in the Holy Spirit* declared" (Mark 12:36). After Peter and John are released from the Sanhedrin in Acts 4 and return to their fellow Christians, they all cry out in prayer, citing Psalm 2. But their view of the psalm is quite plain. They said, "*Sovereign Lord*, who made the heaven and the earth and the sea and everything in them, who through the mouth of our father David, your servant, *said by the Holy Spirit . . .*" (Acts 4:25). These illustrations validate the fact that the early Christians did not understand the Psalms simply as reactions of men to God, but as God's very Word breathed out.

The richness and vitality of the Psalter is seen in the fact that it has held a special place in the heart of the church throughout her history. The church has continued to find great solace in the Psalms as they go through various trials. Those who experience the "dark night of the soul" can run to the psalms that cry out to God and plead with the psalmist for the Lord to not hide His face from them (Ps. 13:1). Those who are in awe at the wonder and beauty of the creation around them, like the psalmist, can praise the Lord for all His awesome works! Praise Him for His excellent greatness! (Ps. 150:2). The beauty of the Psalter is that it contains a vast array of emotions that the people of God experience in their Christian life. Contrary to what passes today as "worship music" where everything is "happy clappy" and people must always have a smile on their face, the psalms remind us that the people of God do not always walk around with this arbitrary grin as if everything is okay. No, Christians still experience deep-seated pain in life. There are real trials, real challenges, and the Psalms help us see that under the inspiration of the Spirit, God's people of old went through those same kinds of difficulties as well. Thus, when we sing the psalms, we hear of the joy, fear, pain, worry, doubt, righteous anger, and overall desire to see God vindicate His name, which resonates deeply with our experiences as pilgrims residing in a foreign land.

While the universal church has always appreciated the beauty of the Psalter and has incorporated it in its worship and prayers, in our modern day some psalms have seemed to not "make the cut." To say it another way, some would argue that not all the psalms should be sung or prayed today, particularly the ones that speak out harshly against enemies. Some popular approaches would say that these psalms were for a different time, or only to be used by the old covenant people of God. But the burden of proof rests on them to demonstrate why some of these psalms cannot be sung or prayed today, while the others can. Should the psalms that present "harsh language" and make us uncomfortable at times still be considered relevant for the church today? Should we still be able to sing, and specifically pray, these kinds of prayers today? To that question, we will now turn.

CHAPTER 2

WHAT ARE THE
IMPRECATORY PSALMS?

WHAT WE ENCOUNTERED earlier with our young minister friend is typical of many Christians in their reading of these psalms. They read one and soon realize there is an entire *body* of them. The reality is that this is a specific genre of psalm known as *imprecatory* psalms. The word "imprecation" is derived from the Latin word *imprecārī,* which means "the action of invoking evil, calamity or divine vengeance upon another, or upon oneself, in an oath or adjuration: cursing."[1] Many of these psalms express different pains and sufferings of the writer. They incorporate lament, which is a crying

---

1. J.A. Simpson and E. S. C. Weiner, eds. "Imprecation," in *Oxford English Dictionary,* 2nd ed. (Oxford: Clarendon, 1989), 7:737, quoted in Eugene H. Merrill, Mark F. Rooker, and Michael A. Grisanti, *The World and the Word: An Introduction to the Old Testament* (Nashville: B&H Academic, 2011), 518.

out to the Lord in the midst of trouble.[2] Lament psalms could include dealing with an unspecified enemy, a problem that the psalmist faced, or even the psalmist's issue with God.[3] Several of these passages of Scripture incorporate a complaint to God and often characterize just how desperate the situation is for the author.[4] Many of these psalms are a cry of distress for a particular situation and call for God to bring a solution.[5] Psalms of imprecation are either individual or corporate laments that call on the Lord to bring judgment upon an enemy.[6]

Different Views on the Psalms of Cursing

It should come as no surprise that these psalms have endured a vast array of different interpretations among Christians and non-Christians. Of

---

2. Longman and Dillard, *An Introduction to the Old Testament*, 247.

3. Ibid., 247–248.

4. Walter Brueggemann, *The Message of the Psalms: A Theological Commentary* (Minneapolis: Augsburg Publishing House, 1984), 54.

5. Richard P. Belcher, *The Messiah and the Psalms: Preaching Christ from All the Psalms* (Scotland: Christian Focus, 2006), 67.

6. Bill T. Arnold and Bryan B. Beyer, *Encountering the Old Testament: A Christian Survey* (Grand Rapids: Baker, 1999), 310. Laney defines them as "an invocation of judgment, calamity, or curse uttered against one's enemies, or the enemies of God." J. Carl Laney, "A Fresh Look at the Imprecatory Psalms," *Bibliotheca Sacra* (1985): 35.

course, there are those that consider their existence as evidence of the absurdity of the Old Testament. One representative of this view argues that these passages of the Hebrew Bible reveal the Old Testament to be nothing more than a collection of documents preserved by religious fanatics:

> Though ultimately the cause of God is at stake in that judgment, the psalm's conclusion, speaking of the effect of the judgment on the righteous, shows on the other hand the undisguised gloating and the cruel vindictiveness of an intolerant religious fanaticism; it is one of those dangerous poisonous blossoms which are liable to grow even on the tree of religious knowledge and clearly shows the limits set to the Old Testament religion.[7]

While his rhetoric may "pack a punch," the argument presented by the non-Christian will not hold sway over those who understand the Bible to be the Word of God. Yet even among those who would adhere to the Bible as God's Word disagree amongst themselves.

One school of thought argues that although the Bible is God's Word, these psalms are nonetheless problematic. Notably, C.S. Lewis viewed these

---

7. Artur Weiser, *The Psalms: A Commentary*, The Old Testament Library (Louisville: Westminster Knox Press, 1962), 432.

psalms as cries expressing a "spirit of hatred."[8] He described Psalm 137:9 in particular as a "devilish verse" in an otherwise beautiful psalm.[9] He even seemed to indicate that specific verses in the most difficult imprecatory psalms are "diabolical."[10] Lewis used other strong language such as "terrible" or "contemptable" to describe these texts.[11] He felt the tension in the fact that these verses were a part of Scripture and that if Christians were to condone or approve of the "hatred that is there; festering, gloating, and undisguised,"[12] we would be acting "wickedly."[13]

Lewis was not the only Christian that struggles with how to understand these psalms. Others have found it difficult to reconcile these passages with Jesus' teaching to love our enemies.[14] In reference to Psalm 137:8-9, one commentator writes:

> There is no simple solution to problems such as these. But these psalms are not the oracles of God; they are Israel's response to

---

8. C.S. Lewis, *Reflections on the Psalms* (Orlando: Harcourt Books, 1986), 20.

9. Ibid., 21.

10. Ibid.

11. Ibid., 21–22

12. Ibid., 22.

13. Ibid.

14. Peter C. Craigie, *Psalms 1-50*, Word Biblical Commentary (Thomas Nelson, 2004), 41.

God's revelation emerging from the painful realities of human life, and thus they open a window into the soul of the psalmist.[15]

He notes that the specific sentiments described in this psalm are simply "evil."[16] For this particular biblical commentator, these psalms are not speaking the oracles of the Lord but are the psalmist's response to the Lord's revelation.

But for the Christian who understands that all Scripture is breathed out by God (2 Tim. 3:16), this view is untenable. As we noted earlier, it is clear that even the biblical writers themselves understood the Psalms to be the Word of God (2 Sam. 23:2, Mark 12:36).[17] One may object by noting that this refers to the book of Psalms in general, but it says nothing of the precise ones in question. While that may be true, the objection does not take into account the way the Psalms would have been viewed by the early church. It was the Psalter *as a whole* that was inherited by the church. Thus, it was not approached with a "buffet" kind of attitude with the individual determining which psalms were inspired and which ones were not. The entirety of the Psalter was considered to be divine revelation from the God of Israel. Moreover,

---

15. Ibid.

16. Ibid, 41-42.

17. John N. Day, "Imprecatory Psalms and Christian Ethics," *Bibliotheca Sacra* 159 (April-June 2002): 167.

the psalm that Jesus cites as being from the Spirit of God (Ps. 110) is quite intense in its own right. God will "shatter kings on the day of His wrath" and "execute judgment among the nations, filling them with corpses." More specific to the point, the Apostle Peter affirms the inspiration of some of the most notorious imprecatory psalms (Ps. 69; 109) when confessing that the *Scriptures* had to be fulfilled concerning Judas (Acts 1:16).[18] It is hard to consider these psalms "devilish" or diabolical when Peter says that they were "foretold by the Holy Spirit" (Acts 1:16).

Another concern with this view is that it *assumes* the imprecatory psalms express evil emotions and *personal* vendettas against one's enemies. Nonetheless, when one considers the themes that run through this genre of psalm, it will be evident that they actually present high ethical values. Examples include the concern for the honor and integrity of God (Ps. 74:22), the desire for justice and the elimination of injustice in the world (Ps. 58:11), a longing to see God's retributive justice in order that God's enemies would seek Him (Ps. 83:17-18) and an intense hatred for sin (Ps. 139:21).[19] As Calvin noted, "It was a holy zeal for the divine glory which impelled [the author] to summon the wicked to God's judgment seat."[20] It seems clear

18. Ibid.

19. Ibid., 23.

20. John Calvin, *Commentary on the Psalms*, vol. 3

that many of the imprecations in the psalms are actually a longing to see the cause of God established and justice to be met. Yearning for God's will to be done on earth in this sense is not devilish or diabolical.

The controversial nature of these psalms results in other interpretations, of which there is no shortage. Some understand these psalms to be consistent with the Old Covenant but inconsistent under the New.[21] Others say these specific laments are only uttered appropriately through the "lips of Christ and consequently only by His followers through Him."[22] Of course, engaging with all of these arguments here would turn this work into anything *but* a primer. Nevertheless, it is our conviction that none of these views is completely adequate when it comes to dealing *fully* with these texts.[23] In order to

---

(Grand Rapids: Christian Classics Ethereal Library), 59.

21. See Day, "Imprecatory Psalms and Christian Ethics": 167. This view is proposed by Laney, "A Fresh Look at the Imprecatory Psalms."

22. Day, "Imprecatory Psalms and Christian Ethics": 167. This view is proposed by James E. Adams. See Adams, *War Psalms and the Prince of Peace: Lessons from the Imprecatory Psalms*, 2nd ed. (Philipsburg: P&R Publishing, 2016). It was also held by Dietrich Bonhoeffer. See Bonhoeffer, *Psalms: The Prayer Book of the Bible* (Minneapolis: Fortress Press, 1974).

23. The dispensational approach of Laney held that the imprecatory psalms were based on the unconditional covenant that Yahweh made with Abraham and his descendants. He felt that the descendants of Abraham that

get a better handle on these passages, we will move to looking at one specific imprecatory psalm and attempt to understand it in its own context.

---

were included in the Abrahamic Covenant were able to call down these judgments in keeping in line with that covenant (Gen. 12:3). In conclusion, Laney stated, "In light of the fact that the Abrahamic Covenant reflects God's promise to Abraham and his descendants, it would be inappropriate for church-age believers to call down God's judgment on the wicked" (Laney, "A Fresh Look at the Imprecatory Psalms": 44). However, as Day noted, this approach seems to not take seriously the imprecations in the New Testament, as well as testimony of the New Testament that affirms "the enduring validity of the Abrahamic promise for those who embrace Christ through faith (Gal. 3:6-29)." Day, *Crying for Justice: What the Psalms Teach Us About Mercy and Vengeance in an Age of Terrorism.* (Grand Rapids: Kregel Publications, 2005), 30–31. The other view, that David prayed these imprecatory psalms as a forerunner of Christ and therefore it is Christ who actually prays these psalms, also has some problems. The most pressing problem is that it does not answer the question about the psalms of imprecations that are not Davidic or the imprecations expressed elsewhere in both testaments (Day, "Imprecatory Psalms and Christian Ethics": 168).

CHAPTER 3

PSALM 137: OVERVIEW AND EXEGESIS

1 By the waters of Babylon,
there we sat down and wept,
when we remembered Zion.
2 On the willows there
we hung up our lyres.
3 For there our captors
required of us songs,
and our tormentors, mirth, saying,
"Sing us one of the songs of Zion!"
4 How shall we sing the Lord's song
in a foreign land?
5 If I forget you, O Jerusalem,
let my right hand forget its skill!
6 Let my tongue stick to the roof of my mouth,
if I do not remember you,
if I do not set Jerusalem
above my highest joy!

*7 Remember, O Lord, against the Edomites
the day of Jerusalem,
how they said, "Lay it bare, lay it bare,
down to its foundations!"
8 O daughter of Babylon, doomed to be
destroyed,
blessed shall he be who repays you
with what you have done to us!
9 Blessed shall he be who takes your little ones
and dashes them against the rock!*

–Psalm 137

This psalm needs no introduction or title in order for us to know the historical situation it is describing. The first verse reveals the context of a communal lament reflecting on the disaster that befell Israel during the fall of Judah in 586 B.C. The question that we are left with is exactly when this was written. One view is that the author has already returned to Jerusalem and is thinking back to when he was in Babylon.[1] Others think it was likely written during the end of the Babylonian captivity.[2] This is a possible, but it is hard to read this

---

1. Walter D. Zorn, *Psalms Volume 2*, The NIV College Press Commentary (College Press Publishing Company, 2004), 466.

2. Allen P. Ross, "Psalms," in *The Bible Knowledge Commentary*, ed. John Walvoord and Roy B. Stuck (Wheaton: Victor Books, 1985), 890.

psalm and not see that it is "alive with pain."[3] The memory of the destruction of Jerusalem seems to still be in the mind of the psalmist, and the historical situation is a little unsettling.[4] Thus, it is more plausible that the author is writing this psalm close to the time of Jerusalem's destruction and when Jews had settled in Babylon as exiles.

The devastation of Jerusalem by the Babylonians was a historical bloodbath. This invasion wiped out the land and deported the people of God to another. The frightening details that occurred were foretold by the Lord through Moses in Deuteronomy 28:53-57, and the Babylonians were the historical *tool* used by the hand of God. The warfare used by the Babylonians was sickening and harsh. John Day records some of the horrible consequences of covenant disloyalty in siege warfare in the ancient Near East.[5] He quotes from the vassal treaties of Ershaddon:

> May Shamash plow up your cities with an iron plow. Just as this ewe is cut open and the flesh of its young placed in its mouth, so may he make you eat in your hunger the

3. Derek Kidner, *Psalms 73-150*, Tyndale Old Testament Commentaries (London: Inter-varsity Press, 1975), 495.

4. Richard P. Belcher Jr., *The Messiah and the Psalms: Preaching Christ from All the Psalms* (Scotland: Christian Focus Publications, 2006), 76.

5. Day, *Crying for Justice*, 65.

flesh of your brothers, your sons, and your daughters.[6]

He further quotes:

Just as honeycomb is pierced through and through with holes, so may holes be pierced through and through in your flesh, the flesh of your women, your brothers, your sons and daughters while you are alive.[7]

Some of the most gruesome and barbaric acts of this kind of warfare practiced by the Babylonians include the killing of infants inside the womb and taking the babies and throwing them against the rocks.[8] This act insured that the next generation would not be able to rise up and fight. It was in essence a war on the next generation.[9]

This is where we find the author of this text. He is reflecting on the horrible siege that took place and the destruction of the holy land. We find the psalmist by the "rivers of Babylon."[10] Thus, he is settled

---

6. Ibid.

7. Ibid.

8. Ibid.

9. Day, "Imprecatory Psalms and Christian Ethics": 174.

10. "The rivers of Babylon are here those of the Babylonian empire: not merely the Euphrates with its canals, and the Tigris, but also the Chaboras and Eulaeos, on whose lonesome banks Ezekiel (Ezek. 1:3) and Daniel

in the land of Babylon,[11] weeping and reflecting upon the destruction of Zion (Ps. 137:1-2).

Exegesis of Psalm 137

It seems that the best way to approach this psalm is to divide the text into two sections with a sub-heading in the final section. The first section deals with the complaint (vv. 1-4), while the second section deals with the imprecation (vv. 5-9). Within the imprecation itself, we would include both the self-imprecation (vv. 5-7) and the imprecation against the enemies (vv. 8-9).[12]

The Complaint (vv. 1-4)

As noted above, the psalmist is reeling from the pain and destruction he witnessed when the Babylonians crushed Judah and Jerusalem. He is settled in the land of Babylon and weeping over the calamity that befell Zion (v. 1). The writer and his fellow Israelites had no desire to sing the songs of Zion. In fact, they hung their instruments on the trees of the land as an expression of their grief and loss

---

(Dan. 8:2) beheld divine visions." C.F. Keil and F. Delitzsch, *Commentary on the Old Testament*, vol. 5, Psalms (Peabody: Hendrickson, 2001), 800.

11. William A. VanGemeren, "Psalms," in *The Expositor's Bible Commentary*, ed. Frank E. Gaebelein, vol. 5 (Grand Rapids: Zondervan, 1991), 827.

12. Belcher, *Messiah and the Psalms*, 76.

of joy (v. 2). The desire of Israel's captors to hear them sing a song comes in a mocking tone.[13] The "captors" ask them to sing songs for them, most likely referring to any generic "Judean-song,"[14] while their "tormentors"[15] more specifically ask them to recite one of the "songs of Zion" (v. 3). The "songs of Zion" refer to those psalms that would celebrate the glory, splendor, and sovereign protection of the Lord over His people (Ps. 46; 48; 76; 84; 87; 122).[16] Verse 4 sets itself up as a response to the request, "How can we sing the Lord's song in a foreign land?" One of the pressing questions must have been how the Israelites could sing the praises of Yahweh, the God of Israel, while they were unclean living in an unclean land (Amos 7:17).[17] More pointedly, how could the people of

---

13. Some commentators do not see this request as a form of mocking. See James Montgomery Boice, *Psalms: Psalms 107–150*, vol. 3, An Expositional Commentary (Grand Rapids: Baker, 1998), 1188. However, one must ask the question why the captors (Babylonians) would ask them to sing a song that would elevate Yahweh, Yahweh's people and the holy land if it was not for the sole reason of mocking and taunting the Judeans. See John Ahn, "Psalm 137: Complex Communal Laments," in *Journal of Biblical Literature* (2008): 267–289, 281.

14. John Ahn, "Psalm 137: A Complex Communal Lament": 281.

15. Ibid., 282. Ahn has a discussion on the possibility of the "tormentors" and "captors" being distinct groups.

16. VanGemeren, "Psalms," 827.

17. A.A. Anderson, *Psalms 73–150*, vol. 2, The New

Israel sing a song about the Lord's protection and strength while the holy land is in ruins and they are captive in a foreign land?

The Imprecation (vv. 5-9).

The psalmists imprecations consist of two parts, that of self-imprecation (vv. 5-6) and of cursing upon the enemies (vv. 7-9).

Self-Imprecation

When the people of Judah, the southern kingdom in the history of Israel, were exiled to Babylon, there was a strong possibility that they would forget Jerusalem. This was all the more likely as the exiled generation passed on and a new generation arose that did not know Zion. For this reason, we can understand the writer's obstinate desire to not forget Jerusalem. The city of Jerusalem was not just the place that was central to the religion of Israel, but it was the very location where the Lord had met and communed with His covenant people.[18] It was so vital that the psalmist remember everything that the city stood for—the law, covenant, sacri-

Century Bible Commentary (Grand Rapids: Eerdmans, 1992), 899. This was quoted by Ahn, "Psalm 137: A Complex Communal Lament", 282.

18. Craig C. Broyles, *Psalms*, Understanding the Bible Commentary Series (Grand Rapids: Baker, 1999).

fice, atonement, and so forth[19]—that he calls down a curse upon himself to make sure that he does not forget. That the author calls on God to make his right hand "forget her skill" and his tongue to "cling to the roof of his mouth" may suggest that the psalmist was a skilled musician[20] who is calling down a curse for him to be paralyzed and never play or praise again if he forgets the holy land.[21]

Imprecation Against Babylon

So far, up to this point, there is not really an objection. The fact that the author calls down a curse upon himself does not really offend anyone. In fact, people call down "curses" upon themselves for much more silly and shallow things today. What really offends us is the last few verses of the psalm.

The cursing turns from the psalmist himself to the enemies that have destroyed Jerusalem. Yet it is important to realize up front that the curse is *not* against the psalmist's personal enemies but ultimately against the enemies of God, and the desire is to see the cause of God established.[22] Beginning with this self-imprecation, the writer shows that his

---

19. VanGemeren, "Psalms," 828.

20. Ahn, "Psalm 137: Complex Communal Lament": 284. Ahn argues that the author here reveals that he is a Levite. This is quite plausible.

21. Ibid.

22. Belcher, *Messiah and the Psalms*, 79.

ultimate concern is that Jerusalem not be forgotten and that God be glorified in the outcome of this situation. The psalmist is willing to curse himself if he does not bring God glory in remembering Him. Yet God's glory and God's cause also include the judgment of the enemies of the Lord, and it is here that the writer at this point directs his focus.

The author first focuses his attention to the nation of Edom (v. 7). The Edomites, the people descended from Esau, Jacob's brother, desired to see the Israelites destroyed. They even *rejoiced* over the reality of seeing Israel destroyed (Obad. 10-14). The psalmist calls for God to remember what the Edomites had done to His people. Not only does the psalmist call God to remember what Edom had done but the psalmist calls on God to bring upon them the judgment that the Lord had *already revealed He would bring* (Jer. 49:7-22; Ezek. 35:1-6). God had revealed that Edom would be laid waste and desolate (Ezek. 35:3) because they gave the people of Israel over to the sword in the day of their calamity (35:5). The psalmist was calling to see God's justice established and His will to be done against the Edomites.

The psalmist then turns his attention to Babylon. Babylon will be devastated and repaid for the atrocities that she has committed. In this verse, the psalmist seems to be referring to the promise of God that He would repay Babylon for her iniquity (Jer. 51:55-56). The psalmist harkens back to the *lex talionis*, something that we will consider in depth in the pages to come. Suffice it to say that the author called for the *repayment* of the Babylonians for what they had done to Israel, a repayment that God had *already* ordained would occur.

It is in verse 9 that the writer unfolds some of the carnage that was inflicted upon Israel by Babylon. He calls for the same infliction to be rendered on the Babylonians. Twice the author mentions how blessed (happy) those who repay Babylon would be (vv. 8-9). The word "blessed" is used twenty-six times in the book of Psalms, and never is it used of a person who is expressing sadistic joy and seeking the personal destruction and ruin of a people for their sick pleasure.[23] This should not be taken as an exception. The psalmist was not calling for his own *personal* revenge against the people of Babylon, but he desired to see come to fruition what God had already revealed would occur.[24] God had revealed that Babylon would be repaid the very same way it had destroyed Israel. The Lord proclaimed that their children would be "dashed to pieces" (Isa. 13:16) and their sons would be "slaughtered" (Isa.

---

23. Walter C. Kaiser Jr., *Hard Sayings of the Old Testament* (Downers Grove: Inter-Varsity Press, 1988), 173.

24. This is contrary to Weiser who says that these words are filled with "blind hate and vulgar rage." The psalmist is certainly angry over what the Babylonians have done to God's land and God's people, yet his anger is in line with the anger of Yahweh and he calls on Yahweh to fulfill what He has already determined would occur. Weiser, *The Psalms*, 796.

14:21). This fact is vital to understand the mindset of the psalmist. He is not calling down these atrocities on *his* enemies out of blind fury and unhinged anger, but calling on God to fulfill *His* prophetic judgments that *He* had promised would occur. He is calling them down in *specificity*. God had said His judgment would include the children of the Babylonians being "dashed to pieces," which is why the psalmist uses that precise language.

At the same time, it should be emphasized that the psalmist was not stoic in his emotions, passively writing the psalm without a tear in his eye. No, this psalm is filled with emotion. It is filled with intense anger, distress, and hurt. We know from Scripture that anger is not always a sinful reaction. Paul exhorts us to not sin in our anger (Eph. 4:26), implying that there is a category of anger that is *not* sinful. We see throughout Scripture where God is angry at the wicked and is a righteous God who has indignation every day (Ps. 7:11). We have an example of righteous anger in the incarnate Son when He cleansed the temple from the profiteers who were making the Lord's house a "den of thieves" (Matt. 21:12-13). Overturning the tables and pushing out the moneychangers was perfectly consistent with Jesus' holiness and righteousness. All of this is to say that the psalmist *was* expressing anger, but it was a holy anger aimed at those who ultimately hated God and wanted to destroy His people. In righteous anger, the psalmist calls down upon the Babylonians the destruction of their children because God had already said that it would happen.

The Theology Behind Psalm 137

In order to grasp this psalm more completely, it is important for us to understand its theological foundation. The basis for the psalmist's claim is not his own bloodthirsty desire to take vengeance, but it is the principle of divine justice that we see expressed in the *lex talionis*.[25] The lex talionis is a reference to the "law of retaliation"[26] and is found in passages such as Exodus 21:22-25, Leviticus 24:17-22, and Deuteronomy 19:16-21. This law sought to prevent the excesses of revenge and to ensure that *personal* revenge did not occur.[27] It was intended to ensure that justice would be accomplished and that the punishment enforced would fit the crime committed.[28] This law is an attribute of any civilized society that makes sure a person is not given a harsher punishment than the crime deserves.

This principle, also known as an "eye for an eye," was more than likely not always carried out *literally* in Israel.[29] In a fair number of cases, such

---

25. Day, *Crying for Justice*, 66.

26. Ibid.

27. Ibid.

28. Ibid.

29. See Joe M. Sprinkle, "The Interpretation of Exodus

as ones related to animals or situations that caused bodily injury, the lex talionis principle would have been a guide for judges to make sure that the punishment would not be harsher than the actual violation.[30] To say it another way, this principle placed restrictions on the kind of punishments that judges could hand out. In some of these cases, the punishment would be in the form of some kind of compensation.[31] For example, "if a slave loses an eye, an eye of the one responsible is *not* to be plucked out but rather the slave is to be given his freedom as *compensation* for the eye" (Ex. 21:26).[32] However, because God placed a high value on human life, as those made in His image, actions resulting in death warranted significant penalty in the codification of the law. This seems to be one of the *only* places where the lex talionis principle was taken *literally*. As one scholar has noted:

> Only in the case of premeditated murder was such compensation forbidden (Num. 35:16). Then the principle of life for life

---

21:22-25 (Lex Talionis) and Abortion," *Westminster Theological Journal* 55 (1993): 233–253.

30. Mark F. Rooker, *Leviticus*, New American Commentary (Nashville: Broadman and Holman Publishers, 2000), 298.

31. Ibid.

32. Ibid.

must be literally enforced because man is made in the image of God (Gen. 9:5-6).[33]

So even though the taking of animal life does not require the person to give up his life, one who intentionally takes the life of a human being[34] is required to give up his life in return (Lev. 24:21).[35] The original intent of this law was judicial, to be executed by the judges of Israel in order to establish *justice* in the nation.

Yet as the history of the nation progressed, so did the understanding of the principle of lex talionis. In Jesus' day the lex talionis was often seen as a way of justifying *personal* revenge. Jesus lived in a world where the people of God were under Roman rule, and it was easy to lose sight of what the original intent of the law was and to begin to understand it as a way to get even with one's personal enemy.[36] But despite the later abuses, the lex talionis was enshrined in Israel's law code in order

---

33. Gordon J. Wenham, *Leviticus*, The New International Commentary on the Old Testament (Grand Rapids: Eerdmans, 1979), 312.

34. Of course, there were distinctions in the law between what we would call "murder," "self-defense," and so forth. The law did not treat someone who murdered an individual the same as one who killed another in battle.

35. Rooker, *Leviticus*, 298.

36. Michael J. Wilkins, *Matthew*, New International Version Application Commentary (Grand Rapids: Zondervan, 2004), 249.

to execute *judicial justice*, not *personal vengeance*. The lex talionis also reflects the character of God Himself. John Day brings this point out effectively:

> Yahweh, although a God of love, is also a God of retribution who deals with his creature's trespasses against his holiness on the basis of his retributive justice. This is seen most clearly and poignantly in the necessity for the Cross. And it is the Cross that both bridges and binds the two testaments. Since it is a grounding assertion that the nature of God does not change (cf. Mal. 3:6; Heb. 13:8), the principle of divine justice based on that nature, as encased in the judicial *lex talionis*, must remain fundamentally constant.[37]

Now an astute observer may fairly ask the question, "This is all informative, but what does it have to do with Psalm 137?" While the discussion of the "eye for an eye" principle may seem like a rabbit trail, it actually helps provide the context for the psalm. The lex talionis is the foundation of this passage. The author is pleading with God to repay the Edomites and the Babylonians for what they had done to Israel. He appeals to the Lord to recompense

---

37. Day, *Crying for Justice*, 68–69. This quote also includes a citation from Bobby J. Gilbert, "An Exegetical and Theological Study of Psalm 137" (Th.M. thesis, Dallas Theological Seminary, 1981), 69.

them with the *same exact* destruction they brought upon God's people, the destruction of their children.[38] By wiping out the children of one's enemy, this would ensure that the next generation would be cut off. From the vantage point of the lex talionis, in seeing the Babylonians repaid by the Lord with a punishment to fit the crime, God's justice would be established and His honor would be upheld.[39]

In conclusion, the cries of the psalmist in this text do not reveal a wicked heart crying out for personal vengeance against an enemy, but they reveal an appeal to the Lord to bring swift judgment and destruction upon the Babylonians according to *His* will and promise (Isa. 13:16; Jer. 51:56; Ezek. 35:1-6). God retains the prerogative to do as He pleases. In His mercy, He has not destroyed us all, even though it is what we deserve as rebel sinners. God reserves the right to do with His creatures what He wills, and even though it may be difficult for us to understand at times, God is still just and holy when meting out His judgment. While it may be difficult for our modern ears to read of such cries, two conclusions suffice:

> In line with ethical standards, Psalm 137:8-9 appeals to Yahweh as the judge supreme to mete out justice according to his own edict. And since in God's economy, no ransom

---

38. Ibid., 70.

39. Ibid.

was to be allowed for murder, the psalmist cries out for the divine judgment of compensatory bloodshed.[40]

The principle of strict judicial retaliation cannot be maligned without maligning the character of God, who both established and promised it.[41]

But Dashing Babies?

Despite the explanation, it is obvious that this kind of image makes us uncomfortable. How can someone truly ask for the dashing of *babies*? For one thing, the translation may be a bit misleading. The term that we translate as "infant" or "little ones" has a bit wider range of meaning, referring to a category of person anywhere from infancy to just prior to mature adolescence.[42] In other words, the term itself does not specify any age.[43] It is possible that this person was older in age, and thus actively participating in the wickedness and moral degradation that was taking place. In other words, the sins of the fathers were being repeated by their children and thus ripe for judgment from God.

---

40. Ibid., 71.

41. Ibid.

42. James A. Swanson, *Dictionary of Biblical Languages with Semantic Domains: Hebrew* (Oak Harbor: Logos Research Systems, Inc., 1997).

43. Kaiser, *Hard Sayings of the Old Testament*, 174.

Nevertheless, despite the age of the one who would be "dashed against the rocks," it is important to reiterate that this is a righteous plea for God to fulfill His prophecy of judgment. God declared that this would befall the Babylonians and He would fulfill it through human instrumentation. So while the psalmist is calling for someone to act in this fashion, specifically He is calling on God to accomplish it through a secondary cause. In the end, if anyone has an issue with this, it is not the psalm or the imprecations in general that is the ultimate problem. Rather it is God who is the object of their disdain since He often works in this fashion, using human beings as a means to bring down His judgment. We see in the book of Joshua that God uses Israel as a tool of judgment to destroy the Canaanites because their iniquity had been filled up (Gen. 15:6). We note that God not only used Israel, but passages such as Isaiah 10 and the book of Habakkuk show us that God often used pagan nations to bring judgment upon an apostate Israel. The point here is that the prophets cry, and God utilizing the nations to execute His *just* judgment is not out of the ordinary but a consistent theme in Scripture. Furthermore, as one theologian has noted: "Righteous retribution is one of the glories of divine character. If it is right that God should desire to exercise it, then it cannot be wrong for his people to desire him to exercise it."[44]

---

44. R.L. Dabney, *Discussions Vol. I: Theological and*

CHAPTER 4

THE IMPRECATORY PSALMS AND THE NEW TESTAMENT

IF WE WANT to establish a connection between the imprecatory psalms and the believer today, we need to spend some time in the New Testament. Is there any reason to believe that the Christian is able to utter these kinds of prayers to God under the new covenant? Or is there a legitimate reason to agree with Old Testament commentators Keil and Delitzsch that a psalm such as Psalm 137 is not suited to the "mouth of the New Testament church"?[1] In our attempt to answer this question, we will consider two issues: (1) Is loving our enemies *compatible* with the psalms of cursing? (2) Are there examples of imprecatory prayers in the New Testament?

Evangelical (Richmond: Presbyterian Committee of Publication, 1890), 715.

1. Keil and Delitzsch, *Psalms*, 803.

Imprecations and Loving our Enemies

Those who would argue that the imprecatory psalms have no place in the vocabulary of the faithful point to Jesus' ethic of loving our enemies. They argue that Jesus' ethic of loving our enemy and not taking revenge contradicts the anger and vengeance of the imprecatory psalms. It seems, however, as one commentator wrote, that comparing this ethic with the imprecations is comparing "apples to oranges."[2] Or to say it another way, we are committing a category error when we make this kind of argument. As observed earlier, the lex talionis was instituted for the purpose of *preventing* private vengeance. The principle of lex talionis took vengeance out of the hand of the offended since the one who committed a crime would receive punishment. However, as much as the law sought to prohibit private vengeance, Jewish tradition tended to include private vengeance as part of the lex talionis.[3] The evolution of Jewish tradition is the context needed to help us understand Jesus' instruction. He was calling for His followers not to give place to personal revenge but to show love to those who seek to harm them (Matt. 5:39-42). In doing this, Jesus brought the Jews back to the foundation of the Old Testament. The Lord had forbidden the Israelites

2. Belcher, *Messiah and the Psalms*, 77.

3. Leon Morris, *The Gospel of Matthew*, Pillar New Testament Commentary (Grand Rapids: Eerdmans, 1992), 126.

from taking personal revenge and instead required them to leave vengeance to *Him* (Lev. 19:18; Deut. 32:35, 41; Prov. 24:29).

In calling the Jews to love their enemies, Jesus was *not* introducing something foreign to the Old Testament law. The Old Testament exhorted the Israelites to show love to their enemies. Although the specific *words* are not utilized, the *actions* of the Israelites were to demonstrate kindness and compassion to an enemy. For example, the Torah expected the Israelites to show assistance to an enemy if he needed aid with his ox or donkey (Ex. 23:4-5). Laws like these were seeds that would ultimately come to fruition in Christ's command of enemy love.[4] Therefore, there was no reason for later Jewish tradition to think that the command to love one's neighbor (Lev. 19:18) implied they were to hate someone who was not their neighbor.[5] Jesus shatters this understanding and breaks down the wall of Jewish tradition that separated one's neighbor and enemy. Jesus taught that someone's neighbor included every human being[6] and not simply someone who loved and cared for them (Matt. 5:44-47; see also Luke 10:25-37). In essence,

---

4. William Hendriksen, *Exposition of the Gospel of Matthew*, New Testament Commentary (Grand Rapids: Baker, 1973), 313.

5. Charles Quarles, *Sermon on the Mount: Restoring Christ's Message to the Modern Church* (Nashville: B&H Publishing Group, 2011), 158–159.

6. Hendriksen, *Matthew*, 313.

Jesus emphasized what the Old Testament already called for in practice, the idea of "enemy love."[7]

The point is that the idea of enemy love was not something radically new and disconnected from the old covenant Scriptures. As was demonstrated, the Old Testament is consistent with the New when it comes to loving enemies. As will be argued below, the New Testament is also consistent with the Old in that it contains *imprecations*. Therefore, at least in *principle*, enemy love and imprecations are not completely incompatible. Otherwise we would have to say that the Old Testament is inconsistent at this point. Those who say there is an inconsistency assume these imprecatory psalms display personal vengeance, which is categorically not the case. These psalms are not personal crusades, but they express a desire to see the Lord's purpose established and *divine* vengeance met out.

New Testament Imprecations

Furthermore, it is not *only* the Old Testament that displays this tension between enemy love and imprecations, but the New Testament does as well. Jesus, the perfect embodiment of enemy love, did not hesitate to speak imprecations (Mark 11:12-14; 20-21) and woes against those that were hardened

---

7. Day, *Crying for Justice*, 89.

in unbelief (Matt. 11:20-24; 23:13-39).[8] As one
commentator has observed:

> By Christ's own example, this enemy love is
> the attitude of readiness to show sustained
> and indiscriminate kindness. If, however,
> the enemy's cup of iniquity has become full
> to overflowing, this love is overtaken by the
> demands of justice and divine vengeance.[9]

One interesting example of this is found in Luke
19:41-44. In this account, we find Jesus entering
Jerusalem. As He draws near the city, He begins
to mourn over the fact that judgment will come
upon the nation of Israel because, as a whole, they
did not recognize Him as their Messiah. National
Israel had rejected Jesus as the Christ, and because
of this, He utters an *imprecation* against them!
The context of this cursing harkens back to Deuteronomy 28–32 and is the result of covenant
unfaithfulness on behalf of the nation.[10] Thus,
amidst Jesus' mourning over the nation for their
covenant unfaithfulness, He calls down a judgment
that God had already purposed would happen to
Israel when they disregarded the covenant and

8. I lean heavily on Day, *Crying for Justice*, 89, for
this insight.

9. Day, *Crying for Justice*, 90.

10. Darrell L. Bock, *Luke*, The New International Version Application Commentary (Grand Rapids: Zondervan, 1996), 494.

rejected Him. Now what is intriguing about this particular passage is that Jesus says that the Jews' enemies will "tear you down to the ground, you and your children within you" (Luke 19:44). The Greek word for "tear down" is ἐδαφιοῦσίν (*edaphiousin*). It can mean to "raze something from the ground" or to "dash something to the ground."[11] Some commentators have argued that Jesus may very well be quoting from the Septuagint version of Psalm 137,[12] the reason being that the very same Greek term is utilized when referring to the babies being "dashed upon the rocks" (137:9).[13] Regardless, is it evident that the Lord Himself had no problem calling down imprecations that were reminiscent of Psalm 137. It seems then, as Day has noted, "rather than being totally incompatible, enemy love and enemy curse are found, strangely, to complement one another."[14]

One may reasonably object that, while true that Jesus uttered imprecations, it does not necessarily follow from this fact that anyone else ought to do so. Jesus was the perfect Son of God. He could utter those because they flowed from a perfect and

---

11. I. Howard Marshall, *The Gospel of Luke*, New International Greek Testament Commentary (Exeter: Paternoster Press, 1978), 718.

12. Psalm 137 is labelled as Psalm 136 in the Greek Septuagint.

13. Kaiser, *Hard Sayings of the Old Testament*, 173–174.

14. Day, *Crying for Justice*, 90.

pure heart. Perhaps this is an example of one of those times where we *cannot* do as Jesus did. At least one problem with this objection, however, is that we find these kinds of imprecations scattered all over the sacred history of the church, including the apostles' epistles in the New Testament.[15] Such language in the New Testament is reserved for those who were seeking to pervert the truth of the gospel. The Apostle Peter, in confronting the magician Simon, utters the curse, "May your silver perish with you" (Acts 8:20). Peter condemns Simon to eternal destruction if he does not turn from his wicked ways and turn to God (8:22-23). The Apostle Paul also was not shy about uttering curses when they were appropriate. We see this when he confronts Elymas the magician who sought to turn the proconsul away from the teachings of Paul and Barnabas. Paul utters words of cursing when he says:

> You son of the devil, you enemy of all righteousness, full of all deceit and villainy, will you not stop making crooked the straight paths of the Lord? And now, behold, the hand of the Lord is upon you, and you will be blind and unable to see the sun for a time (Acts 13:10-11).

---

15. Many of these, as well as other examples, can be found in Day, *Crying for Justice,* 104–107.

Likewise, Paul reserves some of the harshest imprecations in his epistle to the Galatians. He calls down damnation on those that would seek to preach a different gospel:

> But even if we or an angel from heaven should preach to you a gospel contrary to the one we preached to you, let him be accursed. As we have said before, so now I say again: If anyone is preaching to you a gospel contrary to the one you received, let him be accursed (Gal. 1:8-9).

The idea behind the word for "accursed" (ἀνάθεμα, *anathema*) is to devote something to destruction. Paul is invoking *God's* final damnation and wrath on people who would distort the gospel of grace and replace it with the "gospel" of the Judaizers.[16]

Two final imprecations are seen in the last book of the New Testament, the book of Revelation. In various places, Revelation calls for God's justice and judgment to fall upon the ungodly and unbelieving world. In Revelation 6:10, the martyrs cry out to God to avenge their blood. These saints are crying out for the justice of God to be established upon the earth. The martyrs are not crying out for *revenge*, but they are calling out to God to *actualize*

---

16. Scot McKnight, *Galatians*, The New International Version Application Commentary (Grand Rapids: Zondervan, 1995), 51.

what He has *promised* elsewhere. New Testament scholar Simon Kistemaker notes:

> The saints ask God for justice and petition him to avenge them. He himself has said, "It is mine to avenge; I will repay" and "the LORD will judge his people" (Deut. 32:35, 36). This promise is solemn and sure, for God never breaks his word. The possessive pronoun our in "our blood" is telling, for God does not forget the spilled blood of his people and repeatedly utters his warning not to shed innocent blood.[17]

These *sinless* saints are never condemned for their cries for justice and judgment but are instead told by God to "rest a little while longer" (Rev. 6:11). In Revelation 18:20, after the devastation and destruction of Babylon is described, the saints are called to rejoice! While the earth dwellers mourn over the leveling of Babylon, the saints, prophets, and apostles are called to rejoice over her devastation and judgment. God calls for their praise since He judged Babylon to avenge their blood (18:20). What these texts tell us in the Apocalypse is that even though these saints have shed the remnants of indwelling sin, they can still demand and rejoice

---

17. Simon Kistemaker, *Exposition of the Book of Revelation,* New Testament Commentary (Grand Rapids: Baker, 2001), 233.

in the judgment and destruction of the enemies of God that have harmed them.

What seems clear from our brief overview of some of the imprecations in the New Testament is that the command to love one's enemies is not inconsistent with the calls for God to bring vengeance. It seems clear from the data we have in Scripture that there are times where calls for judgment and cursing are warranted and appropriate. And doing so does not put us at odds with the biblical command to love our enemies.

This is at odds with the approach advocated by theologian Michael Horton, who argues that Christians today are not to pray these psalms because we live in the ethical age of common grace. He writes: "The imprecatory psalms, invoking God's judgment on enemies, are appropriate on the lips of David and the martyrs in heaven. However, they are entirely out of place on the lips of Christians today, guided as we are not by the ethics of intrusion but by the ethics of common grace."[18] The most significant problem with this position is it does not take into account the various kinds of imprecations contained in the New Testament that do not fall into the categories of David and the saints in heaven. As we have seen, imprecations have been found not only on the lips of Christ,

---

18. See Michael Horton, *The Christian Faith: A Systematic Theology for Pilgrims on the Way* (Grand Rapids: Zondervan, 2011), 961–962.

but in Peter and Paul as well, and there does not seem to be any contradiction between the imprecations that they proclaim and the "ethic of common grace" in which they lived.

This leads to the second problem, as there is an assumption in this position that the imprecatory psalms stand in stark contrast, if not in contradiction, to the view of neighbor love. But as previously shown, we do not see this in either the Old or New Testament. Rather, we see the concept of love for the unbeliever and the psalms of cursing coming together in a "strange harmony." This position simply does not square with the evidence provided in the New Testament where we find that imprecations are, at times, appropriate for the church to utilize. Of course, the question that still needs to be answered is *when* they are appropriate.

CHAPTER 5

CAN A CHRISTIAN PRAY
THESE PSALMS?

IN A DAY and age where popular evangelicalism is laden with sentimental slogans and feel-good messages, it is hard to fathom that imprecatory psalms could ever have a place in the church. To a Christian populace that prefers Joel Osteen and his smile over Jonathan Edwards and "Sinners in the Hands of an Angry God," the psalms of cursing sound foreign. Nonetheless, if Scripture is our guide, then there ought to be a place for the psalms of cursing in the life of a Christian. Indeed, we must tread these waters with caution and great care. What this *does not* mean is that a Christian may call down imprecations for silly and flippant reasons. A husband should not call down curses on his wife for burning the toast, nor should the Christian wife call on God to take vengeance when her husband forgets to take out the trash. The Bible does not allow us to utilize the psalms of cursing whenever it suits our fancy. That is because the origin of these psalms were not reactions to personal dissatisfaction, but of God's perfect judgment.

Yet the fact that both the Old and New Testaments condemn personal vengeance *and* still both incorporate imprecations leads us to conclude that Christians may (and even should) still pray these psalms today.[1] There may be times when it is appropriate for God's people to call for God's justice to be established and for hard impenitent sinners to receive the reward they are due. One writer puts it well when he says:

> We pray for the conversion of our enemies, but it is also legitimate that we pray for the destruction of those who violently oppose the kingdom of Christ. In this way it is appropriate for God's people today to use the psalms of imprecation, not for personal revenge, but as part of our prayer for the establishment of the cause of Christ.[2]

If it is the case that Christians may pray these psalms, then what are the specific contexts in which they may be expressed? One may think of the horrors of human trafficking. There is an entire *industry* that profits off rape and abuse. The whole pornographic industry makes millions by exploit-

---

1. Belcher, *Messiah and the Psalms*, 78.

2. Ibid., 83.

ing and taking advantage of many. We may rightly call on the Lord to "shatter the teeth of the wicked" who are gleefully profiting from these shattered lives. We may also think of those in the abortion industry who pad their pockets with money made off the murder of infants in the womb. There are people that literally provide food for their families at the expense of baby parts that are bought and sold for research. Praying that their entire production is destroyed and they are held accountable for each and every life they have taken has a place in the Christian prayer circle.

Or one can think of the many situations in which the persecuted church may be able to pray these curses faithfully. Entire segments of the church are subject to some of the most horrific persecution and torture invented by man. Not only would it be appropriate for the persecuted church at times to call on God to bring His vengeance upon the enemies of His church, but as Christians in the West reflect on this horror, we may take up the cause to pray specifically for God to bring judgment upon their persecutors. Perhaps a modern-day example would help:

> This has been the circumstance in Sudan in recent years, in the Islamic government's appalling program of genocide against the Christian population. Similar violent atrocities are standard procedure for terrorist organizations like Al Qaeda, whose leader,

Bin Laden, was the mastermind behind the September 11, 2001 attacks on the United States. . . In such circumstances of real, horrible brutality like that addressed by the psalmist, where there is the pressing temptation to "forget" or abandon the faith for the sake of self-protection (Ps. 137:5-6), this psalm explodes upward. It turns over the matter of justice to the Source of power in the midst of the powerlessness, of hope in the midst of hopelessness.[3]

In times of crises like these, it is a *relief* to shift our focus away from our sinful desire for personal retaliation to the One who has the right of perfect vengeance. God will not let one sin go unpunished and will distribute perfect justice on those that do not know God or obey the gospel.

Perhaps the objection may be put forward that we should be praying for our enemies to know the Lord, to come to Christ, not to be destroyed. Was not the Apostle Paul once an enemy of the church? Imagine if we prayed for God's vengeance instead of God's converting grace? In fact, does not Paul himself tell us in Romans 12 to bless and not curse our persecutors (Rom. 12:14)? This is a fair point and deserves an answer.

First, in regard to Romans 12, the context will help us know how to understand this verse. In

3. Day, *Crying for Justice*, 72.

Romans 12:9, Paul calls on us to abhor what is evil while at the same time blessing the evildoer (Rom. 12:14). The Christian is to seek to live peacefully with all men to the best of his ability (12:18) and leave vengeance to the Lord since *He* will repay the wicked (12:19). Christians are to live peacefully with all men out of confidence that the Lord's justice will be satisfied and the wicked will perish. The people of God are to love their persecutor while entrusting judgment fully in the hands of God. Thus, this passage only confirms what we have argued already, that vengeance is left to the Lord and we are not to take it upon ourselves. Yet as the Bible also asserts, there are times when God's people call upon the Lord to fulfill those curses.[4]

Secondly, this objection misses the argument that is being put forward in this book. We are *not* saying that the only way to respond to intense persecution is to call down God's vengeance. In fact, the normative response should be to pray for God to convert them. We should make a daily effort to pray for the persecuted church and that their persecutors would cease harming them and bow the knee to Christ. However, what we are arguing for is a *recovery* of the prayer of imprecation. We are arguing for the *category*. We are arguing that the prayer of imprecation should have a seat at the table, not for it to be the only thing at the table. In other words, while we want to state that

---

4. See Day, *Crying for Justice*, 85–99.

the psalms of cursing should have a place in our prayers, specifically when we are praying for the persecuted church, it should not be the only type of prayer we pray. It is a both/and, not an either/or type of situation.

Another potential objection is that some of the psalms seem to actually suggest taking revenge on one's own enemies, such as Psalm 41:10 where David calls on God to raise him up to help "repay" those that have wronged him. A legitimate question can be asked as to whether this goes against the general principle of not taking personal vengeance. In response, it is important to keep the context in mind when we consider a psalm like this. David was the king of the covenant nation of Israel. Because of this, calling on the covenant God of the nation to help take vengeance against the enemies of the nation, and by extension David as their leader, would be a valid prayer. The question, however, is whether or not we are in the same position to pray that kind of prayer. In other words, is there a one-to-one correlation in applying this kind of passage to our situation? The short answer is no. We are not kings of a nation in covenant with God, so it would not be appropriate for us to pray against those nations (or people) that are seeking to destroy the nation in which we live. The modern nations where Christians live are *not* Old Testament Israel. They are not in a special covenant with God, and their rulers are not the leaders of God's covenant nation. Those of us in the United

States, for example, should not assume that all our enemies are in the wrong and the U.S. is God's righteous republic. The fact that we have rejected the God who blessed this land so abundantly, and the amount of iniquity we have committed as a country, should make that obvious. However, it is valid to pray against those that are enemies of God and His people. Thus, while we are not taking vengeance on a personal enemy, we are leaving vengeance to the Lord to deal with those that hate Him and His church.

At the end of the day, how do we draw the line in knowing what is acceptable and what is not acceptable? I think a couple of basic principles may help guide our prayers.

First, *what is the motivation for the prayer?* Are these prayers beings offered up out of genuine desire to see God's justice established, or because personal vengeance is lurking in our hearts? Because of sin, we may find ourselves using these kinds of prayers as a cover for personal vendettas. *We* do not like someone or *we* are jealous of a person for a particular reason, and therefore we want to pray for their downfall. These kinds of prayers have no place, and if we find ourselves engaging in this kind of behavior, we ought to first repent and think long and hard before we would even consider praying an imprecatory prayer in the future. On the other hand, some of us may find that we actually have mixed motivation. We have a desire to see God's justice established, *while at the same time* we are struggling with personal vengeance against them. What do we do in this situation? My recommendation would be that, after searching our own heart, if we find that we are harboring bitterness or ungodly anger, then it would be wise to refrain from these kinds of prayers. Imprecatory prayers require the utmost carefulness, and before we come to the Lord with them we want to make sure that they are genuinely out of an earnest desire to see God fulfill His judgment.

Second, *a good rule of thumb is to make these prayers more general than specific.* A great majority of the imprecatory psalms have a more general tone to them. Even when singular pronouns are used, it is often difficult to determine whether a particular individual is being referred to or not. Thus, in keeping with the pattern, it would be preferable to use these prayers more generally rather than aimed at a particular individual. Note when the psalmist prayed in Psalm 137 he was calling down curses on Babylon *as a nation* for their wickedness, not any particular individual. Thus, it is perfectly reasonable to pray that God would bring judgment upon nations, organizations, and groups that are doing things that are completely evil and thus against His holy will. Yet someone may ask, "But do not individuals make up organizations, nations, and groups? Is not the judgment we are calling for going to fall upon actual people, not just a nameless, faceless group?" Yes, but using these prayers in a more general fashion provides an extra layer of protection from us singling out a particular person and causing sinful anger, bitterness, and personal vengeance to gain a foothold in our hearts. It is very easy for us to allow our personal vendettas to get caught up in our prayer of imprecation when it is solely focused on one individual. It is a bit easier to prevent that from happening when our prayers are more generally directed.

Another reason to make our imprecatory prayers more general rather than specific is because it allows for the recognition that God often saves some of the most wicked imaginable. The reality is that *all* of us were dead in sin at one time, and some of us were even participating in some of the most abominable practices ever known. Praying in a more general fashion, as opposed to singling out someone specifically, grants the reality that some of those imprecations that would have fallen on those people actually fell on Christ when He took the covenant curses upon Himself at Calvary. In other words, this principle gives attention to the fact that some of the people caught up in these wicked practices and ripe for judgment are part of God's elect that in time will come to faith in Christ. This reveals that the judgment due to them for their wickedness was actually satisfied when the Son of God stepped off His throne and *legally* took their sin upon Himself. It is hard to read past that sentence without shouting a hearty *amen!*

At the same time, there may be situations when we desire to pray that the Lord would destroy a specific ministry that is positioning itself against the true gospel, or even a ministry centered on a false teacher. How do we pray *generally* for a ministry that is *specifically* centered on one personality? For one thing, there may be times where we take exception to the basic principle of general imprecations. In other words, while praying in generalities should be the norm, some situations may demand we take an exception to the norm. If someone is so blatantly setting themselves up against the gospel, peddling a false message with a large platform that has the potential to damn millions of souls to eternal destruction, there may be a place to be specific. We saw this earlier with Paul when he uttered an imprecation against someone attempting to turn people away from the true gospel Paul preached. We must, however, take great care when exceptions are made. It is not worth praying against a certain individual if we *sin* in the process. But if we can do so with a clear conscience before God, there may be a time to pray an imprecation against an individual who is causing untold harm.

Finally, *it is important to make sure that our imprecatory prayers have a basis in God's judgment.* In other words, is there a clear abomination taking place? The only way to know this is to base it upon the revealed will of God. Clearly, we can see that what occurs in modern-day sex trafficking is a monstrous evil. It is a gross, abominable abuse of the gift of sex that God created and a violation of the dignity and worth of human beings who were created in His image. It is also evident that God will bring judgment upon the sexually immoral and idolaters. We know all of this because it is plain in the text of Scripture. We know this through revelation. Thus, we have a basis for praying that God will bring destruction upon these kinds of people for their evil, and at times we can petition God to bring that to pass. This is very different than praying that God will bring destruction on Johnny because he looked at you the wrong way.

With these kinds of guidelines in place, it is appropriate—and in fact, important—that God's people, the church of Jesus Christ, utilize the imprecations. The cultural decay that we see taking place in the West is ripe for these kinds of prayers.

CONCLUSION

I MAY HAVE stepped on some toes with this book. This work in many ways is hostile to the typical Christian theology that contemporary evangelicals have been schooled in. Modern evangelicalism is ripe with the quality of *niceness*. Just be nice. Have a smile, look warm, and give a hug. Of course, this description is sarcastic, but it gets to the truth of what is behind much of contemporary Christianity. We live in a world where *perception* is what is most important. Christians are expected to make their presence known, commenting on the approved narrative and going out of their way to make sure they do not offend the wrong people. There is no room for the calling down of *true* justice despite the cultural narrative. There is no room for proclaiming what God has already made clear, that those who are outside of Christ stand condemned. Fashionable Christianity leaves no room for Matthew 23—where Christ calls the Pharisees "whitewashed tombs" who are corrupted on the inside and filled with "dead men's bones." It has no room for Paul calling down anathemas on those who attempt to pervert the gospel of Christ, or Jude's condemnation of false teachers (Jude 10-13).

One of the things that made Christians so impactful in the past was the fact that they were willing to call out sin, and they were willing to call upon the God of justice to bring forth that justice on horrific sin. We are losing that at an alarming rate today.

The desire for this book has been to simply put the *idea* of imprecation back into the Christian vocabulary. While we may *never* seek to strike out in personal vengeance against someone who has done us wrong, there may be times when it is appropriate for God's people to call on Him to execute His just retribution on sinners who are blaspheming *His* name and seeking to attack *His* church. What we would say, however, is that if someone has difficulty distinguishing between their own personal desires for vengeance and praying for God's vengeance, then they should not pray them. But for many Christians, a burden is lifted when they look to the Father and cry out for His justice to be done, instead of seeking to do it themselves. May we as the body of Christ seek to be faithful to what the entire counsel of God would teach us in His Word.

A SAMPLE OF IMPRECATIONS IN THE BIBLE

(Italics indicate an imprecation is being uttered)

Psalm 5

Give ear to my words, O Lord;
    consider my groaning.
[2] Give attention to the sound of my cry,
    my King and my God,
    for to you do I pray.
[3] O Lord, in the morning you hear my voice;
    in the morning I prepare a sacrifice for
    you and watch.
[4] *For you are not a God who delights in wickedness;*
    evil may not dwell with you.
[5] *The boastful shall not stand before your eyes;*
    you hate all evildoers.
[6] *You destroy those who speak lies;*
    the Lord abhors the bloodthirsty and deceitful man.

⁷ But I, through the abundance of your steadfast love,
  will enter your house.
I will bow down toward your holy temple
  in the fear of you.
⁸ Lead me, O Lord, in your righteousness
  because of my enemies;
  make your way straight before me.
⁹ *For there is no truth in their mouth;*
  their inmost self is destruction;
their throat is an open grave;
  they flatter with their tongue.
¹⁰ *Make them bear their guilt, O God;*
  let them fall by their own counsels;
because of the abundance of their transgressions cast
them out,
  for they have rebelled against you.
¹¹ But let all who take refuge in you rejoice;
  let them ever sing for joy,
and spread your protection over them,
  that those who love your name may exult in you.
¹² For you bless the righteous, O Lord;
  you cover him with favor as with a shield.

Psalm 11

In the Lord I take refuge;
how can you say to my soul,
  "Flee like a bird to your mountain,
² for behold, the wicked bend the bow;
  they have fitted their arrow to the string
  to shoot in the dark at the upright in heart;

³ if the foundations are destroyed,
   what can the righteous do?"
⁴ The Lord is in his holy temple;
   the Lord's throne is in heaven;
   his eyes see, his eyelids test the children of man.
⁵ *The Lord tests the righteous,*
   but his soul hates the wicked and the one who loves
   violence.
⁶ *Let him rain coals on the wicked;*
   fire and sulfur and a scorching wind shall be the
   portion of their cup.
⁷ *For the Lord is righteous;*
he loves righteous deeds;
   the upright shall behold his face.

Psalm 12

Save, O Lord, for the godly one is gone;
   for the faithful have vanished from among the
   children of man.
² Everyone utters lies to his neighbor;
   with flattering lips and a double heart they speak.
³ *May the Lord cut off all flattering lips,*
   the tongue that makes great boasts,
⁴ *those who say, "With our tongue we will prevail,*
   our lips are with us; who is master over us?"
⁵ "Because the poor are plundered, because the needy
   groan,
   I will now arise," says the Lord;
   "I will place him in the safety for which he longs."
⁶ The words of the Lord are pure words,

like silver refined in a furnace on the ground,
  purified seven times.
[7] You, O Lord, will keep them;
  you will guard us[l] from this generation forever.
[8] On every side the wicked prowl,
  as vileness is exalted among the children of man.

Psalm 36

Transgression speaks to the wicked
  deep in his heart;
there is no fear of God
  before his eyes.
[2] For he flatters himself in his own eyes
  that his iniquity cannot be found out and hated.
[3] The words of his mouth are trouble and deceit;
  he has ceased to act wisely and do good.
[4] He plots trouble while on his bed;
  he sets himself in a way that is not good;
  he does not reject evil.
[5] Your steadfast love, O Lord, extends to the heavens,
  your faithfulness to the clouds.
[6] Your righteousness is like the mountains of God;
  your judgments are like the great deep;
  man and beast you save, O Lord.
[7] How precious is your steadfast love, O God!
  The children of mankind take refuge in the shadow
  of your wings.
[8] They feast on the abundance of your house,
  and you give them drink from the river of your
  delights.

⁹ For with you is the fountain of life;
  in your light do we see light.
¹⁰ *Oh, continue your steadfast love to those who know*
  you,
  and your righteousness to the upright of heart!
¹¹ *Let not the foot of arrogance come upon me,*
  nor the hand of the wicked drive me away.
¹² *There the evildoers lie fallen;*
  they are thrust down, unable to rise.

Psalm 52

Why do you boast of evil, O mighty man?
  The steadfast love of God endures all the day.
² Your tongue plots destruction,
  like a sharp razor, you worker of deceit.
³ You love evil more than good,
  and lying more than speaking what is right. *Selah*
⁴ You love all words that devour,
  O deceitful tongue.
⁵ *But God will break you down forever;*
  he will snatch and tear you from your tent;
  he will uproot you from the land of the living. Selah
⁶ *The righteous shall see and fear,*
  and shall laugh at him, saying,
⁷ *"See the man who would not make*
  God his refuge,
but trusted in the abundance of his riches
  and sought refuge in his own destruction!"
⁸ But I am like a green olive tree
  in the house of God.

I trust in the steadfast love of God
    forever and ever.
9 I will thank you forever,
    because you have done it.
I will wait for your name, for it is good,
    in the presence of the godly.

Psalm 69

Save me, O God!
    For the waters have come up to my neck.
2 I sink in deep mire,
    where there is no foothold;
I have come into deep waters,
    and the flood sweeps over me.
3 I am weary with my crying out;
    my throat is parched.
My eyes grow dim
    with waiting for my God.
4 More in number than the hairs of my head
    are those who hate me without cause;
mighty are those who would destroy me,
    those who attack me with lies.
What I did not steal
    must I now restore?
5 O God, you know my folly;
    the wrongs I have done are not hidden from you.
6 Let not those who hope in you be put to shame
    through me,
    O Lord God of hosts;
let not those who seek you be brought to dishonor

through me,
O God of Israel.
⁷ For it is for your sake that I have borne reproach,
that dishonor has covered my face.
⁸ I have become a stranger to my brothers,
an alien to my mother's sons.
⁹ For zeal for your house has consumed me,
and the reproaches of those who reproach you have
fallen on me.
¹⁰ When I wept and humbled my soul with fasting,
it became my reproach.
¹¹ When I made sackcloth my clothing,
I became a byword to them.
¹² I am the talk of those who sit in the gate,
and the drunkards make songs about me.
¹³ But as for me, my prayer is to you, O Lord.
At an acceptable time, O God,
in the abundance of your steadfast love answer me in
your saving faithfulness.
¹⁴ Deliver me
from sinking in the mire;
let me be delivered from my enemies
and from the deep waters.
¹⁵ Let not the flood sweep over me,
or the deep swallow me up,
or the pit close its mouth over me.
¹⁶ Answer me, O Lord, for your steadfast love is good;
according to your abundant mercy, turn to me.
¹⁷ Hide not your face from your servant,
for I am in distress; make haste to answer me.

¹⁸ Draw near to my soul, redeem me;
  ransom me because of my enemies!
¹⁹ You know my reproach,
  and my shame and my dishonor;
  my foes are all known to you.
²⁰ Reproaches have broken my heart,
  so that I am in despair.
I looked for pity, but there was none,
  and for comforters, but I found none.
²¹ They gave me poison for food,
  and for my thirst they gave me sour wine to drink.
²² *Let their own table before them become a snare;*
  and when they are at peace, let it become a trap.
²³ *Let their eyes be darkened, so that they cannot see,*
  and make their loins tremble continually.
²⁴ *Pour out your indignation upon them,*
  and let your burning anger overtake them.
²⁵ *May their camp be a desolation;*
  let no one dwell in their tents.
²⁶ *For they persecute him whom you have struck down,*
  and they recount the pain of those you have
  wounded.
²⁷ *Add to them punishment upon punishment;*
  may they have no acquittal from you.
²⁸ *Let them be blotted out of the book of the living;*
  let them not be enrolled among the righteous.
²⁹ But I am afflicted and in pain;
  let your salvation, O God, set me on high!
³⁰ I will praise the name of God with a song;
  I will magnify him with thanksgiving.
³¹ This will please the Lord more than an ox

or a bull with horns and hoofs.

32 When the humble see it they will be glad;
    you who seek God, let your hearts revive.
33 For the Lord hears the needy
    and does not despise his own people who
    are prisoners.
34 Let heaven and earth praise him,
    the seas and everything that moves in them.
35 For God will save Zion
    and build up the cities of Judah,
and people shall dwell there and possess it;
36 the offspring of his servants shall inherit it,
    and those who love his name shall dwell in it.

Psalm 79

O God, the nations have come into your inheritance;
    they have defiled your holy temple;
    they have laid Jerusalem in ruins.
2 They have given the bodies of your servants
    to the birds of the heavens for food,
    the flesh of your faithful to the beasts of the earth.
3 They have poured out their blood like water
    all around Jerusalem,
    and there was no one to bury them.
4 We have become a taunt to our neighbors,
    mocked and derided by those around us.
5 *How long, O Lord? Will you be angry forever?*
    Will your jealousy burn like fire?
6 *Pour out your anger on the nations*
    that do not know you,

and on the kingdoms
    that do not call upon your name!
[7] *For they have devoured Jacob*
    and laid waste his habitation.
[8] Do not remember against us our former iniquities;
    let your compassion come speedily to meet us,
    for we are brought very low.
[9] Help us, O God of our salvation,
    for the glory of your name;
deliver us, and atone for our sins,
    for your name's sake!
[10] *Why should the nations say,*
    "Where is their God?"
Let the avenging of the outpoured blood of your
    servants
    be known among the nations before our eyes!
[11] *Let the groans of the prisoners come before you;*
    according to your great power, preserve
    those doomed to die!
[12] *Return sevenfold into the lap of our neighbors*
    the taunts with which they have taunted you, O
    Lord!
[13] But we your people, the sheep of your pasture,
    will give thanks to you forever;
    from generation to generation we will recount
    your praise.

Psalm 94

O Lord, God of vengeance,
    O God of vengeance, shine forth!

² *Rise up, O judge of the earth;*
  repay to the proud what they deserve!
³ *O Lord, how long shall the wicked,*
  how long shall the wicked exult?
⁴ *They pour out their arrogant words;*
  all the evildoers boast.
⁵ *They crush your people, O Lord,*
  and afflict your heritage.
⁶ *They kill the widow and the sojourner,*
  and murder the fatherless;
⁷ *and they say, "The Lord does not see;*
  the God of Jacob does not perceive."
⁸ Understand, O dullest of the people!
  Fools, when will you be wise?
⁹ He who planted the ear, does he not hear?
  He who formed the eye, does he not see?
¹⁰ He who disciplines the nations, does he not rebuke?
  He who teaches man knowledge—
¹¹   the Lord—knows the thoughts of man,
  that they are but a breath.
¹² Blessed is the man whom you discipline, O Lord,
  and whom you teach out of your law,
¹³ to give him rest from days of trouble,
  until a pit is dug for the wicked.
¹⁴ For the Lord will not forsake his people;
  he will not abandon his heritage;
¹⁵ for justice will return to the righteous,
  and all the upright in heart will follow it.
¹⁶ Who rises up for me against the wicked?
  Who stands up for me against evildoers?
¹⁷ If the Lord had not been my help,

my soul would soon have lived in the land of silence.
¹⁸ When I thought, "My foot slips,"
    your steadfast love, O Lord, held me up.
¹⁹ When the cares of my heart are many,
    your consolations cheer my soul.
²⁰ Can wicked rulers be allied with you,
    those who frame injustice by statute?
²¹ They band together against the life of the righteous
    and condemn the innocent to death.
²² *But the Lord has become my stronghold,*
    and my God the rock of my refuge.
²³ *He will bring back on them their iniquity*
    and wipe them out for their wickedness;
    the Lord our God will wipe them out.

Psalm 109

Be not silent, O God of my praise!
² For wicked and deceitful mouths are opened against
    me,
    speaking against me with lying tongues.
³ They encircle me with words of hate,
    and attack me without cause.
⁴ In return for my love they accuse me,
    but I give myself to prayer.
⁵ So they reward me evil for good,
    and hatred for my love.
⁶ *Appoint a wicked man against him;*
    let an accuser stand at his right hand.
⁷ *When he is tried, let him come forth guilty;*
    let his prayer be counted as sin!

⁸ May his days be few;
   may another take his office!
⁹ May his children be fatherless
   and his wife a widow!
¹⁰ May his children wander about and beg,
   seeking food far from the ruins they inhabit!
¹¹ May the creditor seize all that he has;
   may strangers plunder the fruits of his toil!
¹² Let there be none to extend kindness to him,
   nor any to pity his fatherless children!
¹³ May his posterity be cut off;
   may his name be blotted out in the second
   generation!
¹⁴ May the iniquity of his fathers be remembered before
   the Lord,
   and let not the sin of his mother be blotted out!
¹⁵ Let them be before the Lord continually,
   that he may cut off the memory of them from
   the earth!
¹⁶ For he did not remember to show kindness,
   but pursued the poor and needy
   and the brokenhearted, to put them to death.
¹⁷ He loved to curse; let curses come upon him!
   He did not delight in blessing; may it be far from
   him!
¹⁸ He clothed himself with cursing as his coat;
   may it soak into his body like water,
   like oil into his bones!
¹⁹ May it be like a garment that he wraps around him,
   like a belt that he puts on every day!

²⁰ *May this be the reward of my accusers from the Lord,*
   of those who speak evil against my life!
²¹ But you, O God my Lord,
   deal on my behalf for your name's sake;
   because your steadfast love is good, deliver me!
²² For I am poor and needy,
   and my heart is stricken within me.
²³ I am gone like a shadow at evening;
   I am shaken off like a locust.
²⁴ My knees are weak through fasting;
   my body has become gaunt, with no fat.
²⁵ I am an object of scorn to my accusers;
   when they see me, they wag their heads.
²⁶ *Help me, O Lord my God!*
   Save me according to your steadfast love!
²⁷ *Let them know that this is your hand;*
   you, O Lord, have done it!
²⁸ *Let them curse, but you will bless!*
   They arise and are put to shame, but your servant
   will be glad!
²⁹ *May my accusers be clothed with dishonor;*
   may they be wrapped in their own shame as in
   a cloak!
³⁰ With my mouth I will give great thanks to the Lord;
   I will praise him in the midst of the throng.
³¹ For he stands at the right hand of the needy one,
   to save him from those who condemn his soul to
   death.

Matthew 23:1-36

Then Jesus said to the crowds and to his disciples, [2] "The scribes and the Pharisees sit on Moses' seat, [3] so do and observe whatever they tell you, but not the works they do. For they preach, but do not practice. [4] They tie up heavy burdens, hard to bear, and lay them on people's shoulders, but they themselves are not willing to move them with their finger. [5] They do all their deeds to be seen by others. For they make their phylacteries broad and their fringes long, [6] and they love the place of honor at feasts and the best seats in the synagogues [7] and greetings in the marketplaces and being called rabbi by others. [8] But you are not to be called rabbi, for you have one teacher, and you are all brothers. [9] And call no man your father on earth, for you have one Father, who is in heaven. [10] Neither be called instructors, for you have one instructor, the Christ. [11] The greatest among you shall be your servant. [12] Whoever exalts himself will be humbled, and whoever humbles himself will be exalted.

[13] *"But woe to you, scribes and Pharisees, hypocrites*! For you shut the kingdom of heaven in people's faces. For you neither enter yourselves nor allow those who would enter to go in. [15] *Woe to you, scribes and Pharisees, hypocrites!* For you travel across sea and land to make a single proselyte, and when he becomes a proselyte, you make him twice as much a child of hell as yourselves.

[16] *"Woe to you, blind guides*, who say, 'If anyone swears by the temple, it is nothing, but if anyone

swears by the gold of the temple, he is bound by his oath.' [17] You blind fools! For which is greater, the gold or the temple that has made the gold sacred? [18] And you say, 'If anyone swears by the altar, it is nothing, but if anyone swears by the gift that is on the altar, he is bound by his oath.' [19] You blind men! For which is greater, the gift or the altar that makes the gift sacred? [20] So whoever swears by the altar swears by it and by everything on it. [21] And whoever swears by the temple swears by it and by him who dwells in it. [22] And whoever swears by heaven swears by the throne of God and by him who sits upon it.

[23] *"Woe to you, scribes and Pharisees, hypocrites!* For you tithe mint and dill and cumin, and have neglected the weightier matters of the law: justice and mercy and faithfulness. These you ought to have done, without neglecting the others. [24] You blind guides, straining out a gnat and swallowing a camel!

[25] *" Woe to you, scribes and Pharisees, hypocrites*! For you clean the outside of the cup and the plate, but inside they are full of greed and self-indulgence. [26] You blind Pharisee! First clean the inside of the cup and the plate, that the outside also may be clean.

[27] *"Woe to you, scribes and Pharisees, hypocrites! For you are like whitewashed tombs, which outwardly appear beautiful, but within are full of dead people's bones and all uncleanness.* [28] So you also outwardly appear righteous to others, but within you are full of hypocrisy and lawlessness.

[29] *" Woe to you, scribes and Pharisees, hypocrites!* For you build the tombs of the prophets and decorate

the monuments of the righteous, [30] saying, 'If we had lived in the days of our fathers, we would not have taken part with them in shedding the blood of the prophets.' [31] Thus you witness against yourselves that you are sons of those who murdered the prophets. [32] Fill up, then, the measure of your fathers. [33] *You serpents, you brood of vipers, how are you to escape being sentenced to hell?* [34] Therefore I send you prophets and wise men and scribes, some of whom you will kill and crucify, and some you will flog in your synagogues and persecute from town to town, [35] *so that on you may come all the righteous blood shed on earth, from the blood of righteous Abel to the blood of Zechariah the son of Barachiah, whom you murdered between the sanctuary and the altar.* [36] *Truly, I say to you, all these things will come upon this generation.*

Luke 19:41-44

[41] And when he drew near and saw the city, he wept over it, [42] saying, "Would that you, even you, had known on this day the things that make for peace! But now they are hidden from your eyes. [43] *For the days will come upon you, when your enemies will set up a barricade around you and surround you and hem you in on every side* [44] *and tear you down to the ground, you and your children within you. And they will not leave one stone upon another in you, because you did not know the time of your visitation."*

Acts 8:18-20

[18] Now when Simon saw that the Spirit was given through the laying on of the apostles' hands, he offered them money, [19] saying, "Give me this power also, so that anyone on whom I lay my hands may receive the Holy Spirit." [20] *But Peter said to him, "May your silver perish with you, because you thought you could obtain the gift of God with money*! [21] You have neither part nor lot in this matter, for your heart is not right before God.

Acts 13:8-11

[8] But Elymas the magician (for that is the meaning of his name) opposed them, seeking to turn the proconsul away from the faith. [9] But Saul, who was also called Paul, filled with the Holy Spirit, looked intently at him [10] and said, *"You son of the devil, you enemy of all righteousness, full of all deceit and villainy, will you not stop making crooked the straight paths of the Lord? [11] And now, behold, the hand of the Lord is upon you, and you will be blind and unable to see the sun for a time." Immediately mist and darkness fell upon him, and he went about seeking people to lead him by the hand.*

Galatians 1:8-9

[8] *But even if we or an angel from heaven should preach to you a gospel contrary to the one we preached to*

you, let him be accursed. ⁹ As we have said before, so now I say again: If anyone is preaching to you a gospel contrary to the one you received, let him be accursed.

Galatians 5:7-12

⁷ You were running well. Who hindered you from obeying the truth? ⁸ This persuasion is not from him who calls you. ⁹ A little leaven leavens the whole lump. ¹⁰ I have confidence in the Lord that you will take no other view, and the one who is troubling you will bear the penalty, whoever he is. ¹¹ But if I, brothers, still preach circumcision, why am I still being persecuted? *In that case the offense of the cross has been removed. ¹² I wish those who unsettle you would emasculate themselves!*

Jude 10-13

¹⁰ But these people blaspheme all that they do not understand, and they are destroyed by all that they, like unreasoning animals, understand instinctively. *¹¹ Woe to them!* For they walked in the way of Cain and abandoned themselves for the sake of gain to Balaam's error and perished in Korah's rebellion. ¹² These are hidden reefs at your love feasts, as they feast with you without fear, shepherds feeding themselves; waterless clouds, swept along by winds; fruitless trees in late autumn, twice dead, uprooted; ¹³ wild waves of the sea, casting up the foam of their own shame; wandering

stars, *for whom the gloom of utter darkness has been reserved forever.*

Revelation 6:9-11

[9] When he opened the fifth seal, I saw under the altar the souls of those who had been slain for the word of God and for the witness they had borne. [10] *They cried out with a loud voice, "O Sovereign Lord, holy and true, how long before you will judge and avenge our blood on those who dwell on the earth?"* [11] Then they were each given a white robe and told to rest a little longer, until the number of their fellow servants and their brothers should be complete, who were to be killed as they themselves had been.

Made in the USA
Coppell, TX
22 November 2021

66017039R00056